ideals®
THANKSGIVING

To find joy in the common things,
To do our best with what life brings,
To trust that God will lead the way,
To count our blessings day by day,
To love by sharing and forgiving,
This is the secret of thanksgiving.

—ESTHER F. THOM

IDEALS PUBLICATIONS

NASHVILLE, TENNESSEE

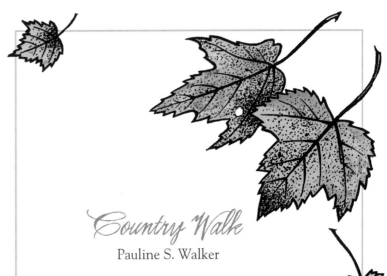

Country Walk

Pauline S. Walker

This is a day for walking in the country . . .
For scuffling roadside drifts of fallen leaves,
For leaving the city cares and city sidewalks;
To find the magic autumn always weaves
With glint of goldenrod and flame of sumac,
With distant wreaths of smoke that lift the eyes
To clouds, like cotton candy, slowly climbing
Into the burnished blue of peaceful skies.

This is a day for remembrance,
For storing lovely keepsakes in the mind . . .
A Monarch butterfly in flight unhurried
To join the fall migration of his kind,
Wild asters fringing wide and sunny meadows
Where placid cattle graze or rest at will,
A field of sunflowers flaunting golden splendor,
A grove of maples blazing on a hill.

How wonderful to walk along the way
Where beauty burns this glorious autumn day!

Photograph by Steve Terrill

The New Expanse of Autumn

Hal Borland

Everybody should own a tree at this time of year. Or a valley full of trees, or a whole hillside. Not legally, in the formal "know all men" way, written on a piece of paper, but in the way that one comes to own a tree by seeing it at the turn of the road, or down the street, or in a park, and watching it day after day and seeing color come to its leaves. That way it is your tree forever, any time you choose to pass that way, and neither fence nor title can take it from you.

I once owned a red maple that way. It stood at the turn of a road I drove along every day, and it was a tree of wonder, for it turned red and gold each year in a different combination. And once I owned a clump of flowering dogwood at the roadside. I watched it bloom in the spring and grow through the summer and deck itself with lacquered berries in September and turn wonderfully crimson in October. I own a whole valley in the Rockies, a valley full of quaking aspens, which I have seen slim and white of bole in winter, and laced with green in spring, and like a flow of molten gold down the mountainside in October.

I have come to own a row of maples along the river here, where I have sat in their June shade and watched them shed their seed, and seen their stark reality in leafless winter. Now I revel in their gold, which is like sunlight even on an overcast day, and before long I shall scuffle in their leaves and own them that way. My ownership is beyond legal title. Others may own them too. Trees are anyone's for the finding, to own forever. . . .

Even as the autumn days shorten they increase in height and breadth. It is as though there were a constant ratio which keeps the days in balance. The leaves are thinning out. The eye can reach. New vistas open. The horizon is just there beyond the trees on the other side of my river, now that the leaves have fallen. The sun slants in a window where two weeks ago there was thick maple shade.

The hills are no longer remote, and at night I can look up from almost anywhere and see the constellations of Andromeda and Pegasus. Even in a land of trees, we are no longer canopied from the sky or walled in from the horizon. The earth's distances invite the eye. And as the eye reaches, so must the mind stretch to meet these new horizons.

True, they are not new horizons; they have been there always. But the very fact that they seem new now, if only because newly seen, is human reason enough for the seasonal succession. Men blind their lives and thoughts by too many walls and canopies, at best. It is good to have the walls and canopies thin away, from time to time, and reveal the broader scope. It is good to be reminded that not only have the days changed, but life itself is a matter of more than two dimensions.

Autumn is an eternal corrective. It is ripeness and color and a time of completion; but it is also breadth and depth and distance. I challenge anyone to stand with autumn on a hilltop and fail to see a new expanse not only around him, but in him too.

Photograph by William H. Johnson

Bright Leaves Afire

John Manier

The leaves ablaze glide down,
Fluttering wildly, flaming round,
Caught within the whirling clown
Of wind, before the touching ground.

Their colors fire the haze—
A miniature sunset glows;
And brings to our rapt gaze
A rain of rainbows.

Wading

Hilda Sanderson

Go wading in the forest
When its floor is golden laid,
And see the splashing autumn leaves
Sailing through the glade.
Look up and see an autumn sky
Above a harvest sea,
Of leaves that fall like colored rain
That patters playfully.

Photograph by Terry Donnelly/
Austin Donnelly Photography

Featured Poet

Blest, Thanksgiving

Eileen Spinelli

Blest are the geese who take their flight
across the sky in golden light.
Blest is the air so apple-sweet,
the leaves that skip along the street,
the pumpkins piled against the wall,
the hum of bees, the blackbirds' call.
Blest are the flowers blooming late,
the sheep asleep beyond the gate,
the wheat, the corn, the lake, the tree . . .
Blest is the earth,
and blest are we.

AUTUMN PATCHWORK *by Diane Phalen.*
Copyright © 2008 by Diane Phalen Watercolors

DIANE PHALEN©

Autumn and the Five Senses

Maxine McCray Miller

Autumn is a time for seeing the glory of living color; the red and gold of hills and dales; the multicolored corn peeping from the shock; the orange of fine pumpkins; the delicate white lace of frost traced on the windowpanes; brown pinecones nestled in the green of pines; scarlet bittersweet berries; purple grapes; the gold of a harvest moon and jack-o'-lanterns with amber lights. It is a time for seeing witches, goblins, ghosts, and skipping gnomes and Mother making jam and jelly.

Autumn is a time for hearing wind that drums a tune on rooftops; the whirring wings of startled quail; the chatter of squirrels hiding nuts away; school bells, school buses, and school lessons. It is a time for hearing the crackle of hay as kittens cuddle down in nests for warmth; the turn of grinders making apple cider; the fiddle playing at the harvest dance; the call of highways leading to fall panoramas and happy songs ringing around campfires.

Autumn is a time for tasting tantalizing pumpkin and mince pies; rich, crunchy nuts; boxed school lunches, fall banquets, and lamplit family dinners. It is a time for tasting trick-or-treat candy, Thanksgiving turkey, and new recipes gathered from the girls at the church supper.

Autumn is a time for smelling the smoke of Indian summer and burning leaves; the fragrance of crystanthemums; the pungent pine in fireplaces; the musky odor of foliage in damp woodlands; the spicy air of kitchens; sweet clover in haylofts and that strange, illusive aroma that tells the person close to nature that the first snow is on the way.

Autumn is a time for touching dreams of hand and heart and gathering their reality; the ripened grain; the gratified shining vision; the luscious peach and apple . . . hope for tomorrow; the realization of the goodness of friends, family, and God. It is a time for touching the coins of labor and love and the edge of infinity . . . the time we come to know in grateful hearts that in this hour of reaping we have again harvested golden fruits of a living faith and its abundant fulfillment.

A Season to Remember

Bernice Peers

Today I walked a garden path
To feast of harvest scene,
To hold within my heart
Before winter does convene.

A tinge of autumn air
Inspired my treasure quest;
Glorified trees, emblazoned leaf
Gave first of vision blest.

Hither and yon, a rabbit
Scurried at fast pace
Busy building winter home
Now that Fall had shown her face.

Pumpkin, squash, and melon
Sparkled in the sun;
Hedge apple, Indian corn,
Pheasant on the run.

A farmer's house, a barn,
The glint of golden grain,
Fireplace log, and chestnut
Gave proof of weathervane.

Coming to the end of path
Restored of autumn's gold,
I thanked God for these gifts
And now let winter scene take hold.

Photograph by Dennis Frates

Bits & Pieces

Gratitude takes three forms: a feeling in the heart, an expression in words, and a giving in return.

—*Author Unknown*

Count your blessings, one by one,
At early morn and set of sun,
And, like an incense to the skies,
Your prayers of thankfulness shall rise.

—*Arthur Lewis Tubbs*

Cultivate the thankful spirit . . . it will be to thee a perpetual feast. There is, or ought to be, with us no such thing as small mercies. A really thankful heart will extract motive for gratitude from everything, making the most of even scanty blessings.

—*Author Unknown*

O Lord that lends me life,
Lend me a heart replete with thankfulness.

—*William Shakespeare*

He who thanks but with the lips
Thanks but in part;
The full, true thanksgiving
Comes from the heart.
— *J. A. Shedd*

Then all the trees of the forest
will sing for joy; they will sing
before the LORD . . .
— *Psalm 96:12b–13 (NIV)*

Thou hast given so much to me,
Give one thing more—a grateful heart;
Not thankful when it pleaseth me,
As if Thy blessings had spare days,
But such a heart whose pulse may be Thy praise.
— *George Herbert*

As we express our gratitude, we must never forget that the
highest appreciation is not to utter words, but to live by them.
— *John Fitzgerald Kennedy*

Thanksgiving Time
Elisabeth Weaver Winstead

The sound of merry laughter
Fills our home this holiday.
We feast on nature's bounty
In a tempting, bright array.

Cousins, aunts, and uncles
Are gathered by the score.
To celebrate Thanksgiving,
We could not ask for more.

This treasured harvest food is shared
By those we cherish best,
With happy hearts we bow our heads
In gratitude expressed.

Then when the day is over
And it's time for guests to part,
May the spirit of Thanksgiving
Linger still within each heart.

Homecoming Streets
Helen Harrington

The streets are calling all their people home;
Lights leap up, and smoke from poked-up fires
Signals excitedly to those who roam.
Every house, now perking up, attires
Itself in what will have the most appeal
For hungry husbands, famished boys and girls:
Scents of roasts and vegetables that steal
Out kitchen windows, pie fragrance that curls
Down walks. Almost everything has been done
To make the welcome felt and will be
Complete and right when the returning one
Is met beyond the threshold tenderly
By what all homeward bound have right to know—
A shining smile and a glad hello!

Photograph by William H. Johnson

FEASTING BY CANDLELIGHT

Cindy La Ferle

It was the weirdest thing. A pair of brass candlesticks I'd kept on the top of the curio cabinet had suddenly disappeared. It was the night before Thanksgiving, and, up until then, I was living under the delusion that everything was in fairly good order. My dining room table was polished and set with cloth napkins and my grandmother's china.

But after putting the final touch on my centerpiece, I noticed the two candlesticks were missing. They weren't the ones I'd planned to use—but their absence was a real mystery. Doug swore he hadn't seen them, and our son, Nate, was out with friends that evening.

I'll never know what possessed me to go outside and look through Nate's car, but I did. There, in a small box on the front seat, were the kidnapped candlesticks plus a pair of partially burned black candles leftover from Halloween.

Why on earth would a high-school senior have these items stashed in his car? I could hardly wait for the explanation.

Well, the candlestick thief returned home shortly thereafter, followed by a noisy troop of teenagers. All were in good spirits and looking forward to their long holiday weekend. To my surprise, the topic of the evening was the traditional Thanksgiving meal they had shared that same afternoon in the high-school cafeteria. The feast had been their own idea, in fact, with no prompting from teachers or school administrators. Few parents even knew they'd planned it.

One student brought a large roasted turkey; others brought side dishes, tablecloths, and trimmings. Nate's contribution to the feast was—you guessed it—the pair of candlesticks with the half-burned Halloween candles, which he'd grabbed in his usual rush out the door that morning.

"Why didn't you tell me?" I grilled him. "I would have given you some new candles." I reminded him, too, that he shouldn't remove things from our dining room without asking. To his credit, Nate apologized and then informed me that he'd grabbed the "ugliest, most hideous pair of candlesticks" he could find, to avoid upsetting me.

Hideous candlesticks aside, teenagers never cease to amaze and delight me. Just when you wonder if they'd even care about ceremonial things like candlelight and holiday dinners, they turn the tables on you. That Thanksgiving feast in the cafeteria was one of the last

Nate and his friends would celebrate as the extended family they've become. Like all families, biological or adopted, they were sharing a ritual as ancient as recorded history. Feasting together provides comfort and forges lifelong memories.

It also occurred to me that my candlestick thief is one lucky young man, especially since he's an only child, to have grown up with other youngsters who'd bother to create a holiday meal together. Last week, in fact, another parent told me that the kids enjoyed it so much that they hoped to do something equally festive for Christmas and Easter.

"Family ritual is pretty much anything we do together deliberately, as long as it's juiced up with some flourish that lifts it above humdrum routine," notes Meg Cox, author of *The Book of New Family Traditions* (2003). As Cox points out, anthropologists have yet to discover a human culture that didn't practice rituals. Rituals impart a sense of identity and help us navigate change. Even the simplest routines we practice when our children are

Photograph by Ben Fink/FoodPix/Jupiter Images

very young, in fact, will help them feel grounded and secure.

So it's definitely worth the trouble—using your grandma's silver, setting a nice table, and recreating holiday menus that have special meaning to your family.

Dress up for the occasion and memorize a toast. And always be sure to keep extra candlesticks on hand.

The Twilight of Thanksgiving

William D. Kelley

Before the evening lamps are lit,
While day and night commingle,
The sire and matron come and sit
Beside the cozy ingle;
And softly speak of the delight
Because beneath their roof tonight
Their dear ones all are dwelling.

And when around the cheerful blaze
The young folks take their places,
What blissful dreams of other days
Light up their aged faces!
The past returns with all its joys,
And they again are living
The years in which, as girls and boys,
Their children kept Thanksgiving.

The stalwart son recalls the time
When, urged to the endeavor,
He tried the well-greased pole to climb
And failed of fame forever.
The daughter tells of her emprise
When, as a new beginner,
She helped her mother make the pies
For the Thanksgiving dinner.

And thus with laughter and jest and song,
And tender recollections,
Love speeds the happy hours along,
And fosters fond affections;
While Fancy, listening to the mirth,
And dreaming pleasant fictions,
Imagines through the winds on earth
That heaven breathes benedictions.

AN AUTUMN DAY *by Ann Stookey.*
Image from Applejack Art Partners

THANKSGIVING

Charles Champlin

I can't say with any accuracy at all just how often Mother and Joe and I went to the Masson house for Thanksgiving dinner. Yet memory translates a relative handful of times into always, and I hold almost no other early recollection of the day, except at the house on Vine Street, with Uncle Victor at the head of the table, doing the carving.

We were never an enormous number around the table, a dozen at most, presuming Aunt Lucie Carpenter was still in town after overseeing the grape-picking in her late father's vineyards and had not yet returned to California for the winter, and if an old family friend, Aunt Fannie Larrowe from down Vine Street, had been invited. There were otherwise Uncle Victor's three sisters—Aunts Julie, Tillie, and Josie—my grandmother Nano Masson, Cousin Melanie Masson, and Aunt Leila Masson, whose late husband was a cousin of Uncle Victor and the aunts.

There was a solemn grace, then a clear soup, and then what seemed a ballet of plate-passing and dish-forwarding. . . .

Joe and I were served first and usually allowed to start right away, with frequent interruptions for the dish-passing. It became a small annual joke in a

Photograph by William H. Johnson

family that loved small ritual jokes that when Uncle Victor had loaded the last plate with turkey and stuffing and handed it on, he said, "Seconds, anyone?" At least once, Joe and I had eaten so fast we had cleaned our plates before Uncle Victor had sat down to begin his meal. The rest of the ritual consisted of cries, led by my grandmother, that Uncle Victor should be allowed to sit down and eat something first.

One of the Hammondsport legacies that has hung on into my present life is that, having myself become the carver of the Thanksgiving turkey, I ask, "Seconds, anyone?" as I hand around the last plate. Or, if I don't ask it quickly enough, one of my now-grown children will say, teasingly, "Seconds, please, Uncle Victor." They have heard about the ritual from my childhood, and they love it and have extended the tradition in memory of a small, precise man with pince-nez glasses whom they never knew. The truth is Uncle Victor had it fairly easy. With six children of our own, plus spouses and grandchildren, we have been as many as twenty at the table (or tables), and I've legitimately been asked for seconds before I sat down. I don't mind at all and neither, I realize now, did Uncle Victor.

For These I Give Thanks

Virginia Katherine Oliver

For these I give thanks—
My blessings large
    and small,
The things life daily brings,
I give thanks for all.

For these I give thanks
As each bright day is born,
So humbly I accept
The gift of a new morn.

For these I give thanks—
For this, my native land,

Free people under God
Where patriots loyal stand.

For these I give thanks—
The friendships that I know,
The tried and true and the new
With bonds that stronger grow.

For this I give thanks—
The love of God for man—
And pray to show my love
    each day,
In every way I can.

My Every Day Thanks-giving

Ardis Rittenhouse

The morning sun that awakens me
Makes me thankful I can see;
Loved ones' voices each so dear
Make me thankful I can hear;
Health and strength that get me through
Make me thankful for what I can do;
Faith that does not let me stray
Makes me thankful for each day;
A mind that reasons and is fair
Makes me thankful that I care;
A heart that accepts help from above
Makes me thankful for God's love.

Our Treasured Traditions

A Place at the Table

Jane Howard

Thanksgiving, at our house on Willow Road in Winetka, Illinois, meant the arrival of a happy swarm of guests—typically my father's parents from their farm in Iowa, some cousins from Wisconsin, a war widow from around the corner—enough company, in any case, to set our table for ten or twelve. . . .

Figuring out who was to sit where, and why, was a lesson in the subtle and important arts of diplomacy and social choreography. Our object, on Willow Road, was to make sure everyone had a good time. So we drew a diagram of our table (with all its extra leaves inserted), wrote the name of each guest on a separate slip of paper, and experimented with different designs for the cheeriest seating arrangement.

Which two guests were the most honored, for reasons of seniority or some other distinction, and should therefore sit to the right of Daddy and Mommy? Who was the shiest? Whoever won that title, along with whoever was the newest among us, should be seated next to whichever guests were the likeliest to put other people at their ease. The wittiest should sit where everyone else has the best chance of hearing the jokes.

And was anyone likely to make trouble? Might a feud be brewing among our guests? In our family, as in many, this could happen. Grudge-holding, like wacky humor and bibliophilism, was a trait that persisted throughout the generations. You might think that holders of grudges would give each other a wide berth, but they don't always. Place cards enabled us to position Uncle Francis and Cousin Winifred as far apart as possible if this was one of the years they weren't speaking. (We always kept in mind that the person you sit across from could have just as much effect on your digestive system as the person to your right or left.)

From one Thanksgiving or Christmas to the next, our place cards were rarely the same. We never bought them at fancy stores like Tiffany's, though some families did, or had them engraved with coats of arms or hired calligraphers. When we could, we relied upon the work of my mother's elegant Auntie Grace, our family's itinerant eccentric and designated artist.

Never traveling without her sketchbook, she was easily persuaded to make place card–sized watercolors evoking her travels. . . .

In Auntie Grace's absence, we kids were appointed to design and make the place cards, which not only kept us out of the way but allowed an outlet for our developing artistic talents. From our first crude place cards cut from construction paper and labeled with crayons, we progressed to more elaborate models, displaying our skill as caricaturists. And we weren't allowed to misspell names. Names, my newspaper-reporter father often reminded us, are something people take very seriously.

Some years when enough cousins joined us, we'd either cluster the kids' place cards at one end of the extended table or set up a separate "children's table." In theory (my theory, anyway), generations should intermingle, with people born before 1920, for example, seated next to those born after 1985. But in reality, kids tend to prefer the company of kids. They don't necessarily want to join in discussions of tax reform or recite one by one "what we have to be thankful for since last November."

If the dinner's going to last a good while, as festive dinners tend to, it's smart for the host and hostess to agree that at some point, they'll trade places or arrange for certain guests—every other person, maybe, or all the men—to take new seats before dessert. On the back of their place cards might be written instructions like: "After the salad course, please change places with Johnny O'B."

Now, childhood long gone, I look back over many holiday rituals, some years as a hostess and some as a guest. My happiest Thanksgivings (and Christmases and Easters and Passovers) have involved place cards. We even used them the year when twelve or so of us roasted our turkey over an open fire in a cabin in New Hampshire. By each place that year, at rustic picnic tables, was a card propped next to a tiny pumpkin. Another year, at a dinner within the sound of the surf, place cards were set between small cairns of special stones and shells gathered from the beach. Christmas tree ornaments also make useful props, as do tiny bottles filled with sprigs of bittersweet or holly. . . .

Place cards, I've realized, can be playful or sentimental or both. Sometimes guests are allowed to take them home as souvenirs, sometimes not. In downtown Manhattan, I have friends whose loft has been the site for seasonal festivities over many years. On Easter Sunday, their place cards are eggs dyed long ago in onion juice and decorated with guests' names. As we search for our eggs at the long table (actually several tables joined together), many of us feel related to these hosts, though technically we aren't, because of their genius for making us feel like family.

We gather there, in custom and ceremony, for the same reason friends and relatives gathered for holidays at our house on Willow Road, and our ancestors assembled on the farm in Iowa: to hear grace said or to pause for a silent moment, to be distracted from the uneasy feeling we all have now and then that we're rattling around in a random, uncaring universe. For a while, at tables like these, our place cards show us where we belong. And that's not a small thing.

Join Hands
Margaret Rorke

Let's join hands around the table,
Thanking God that we are able
To be present at His board;
Feeling grateful for His blessing
On the turkey and the dressing
And the harvest we have stored.

Being mindful of life's changes
And how destiny arranges
Where we're born and how we live,
And the magnitude of merit
As a people we inherit,
It is thanks we ought to give.

Firmly press the touching fingers
Till you feel the warmth that lingers . . .
The sensation sweetly odd . . .
That's transmitting pure affection
And a moment's introspection
With our loved ones and our God.

*The table is brimming
with good things to eat;
We're surrounded by family
and friends—what a treat!*
—KARL FUCHS

Photograph by Jessie Walker

Family Reunion

Virginia Blanck Moore

The table's set with Grandma's best,
The silver's shining bright,
The crystal's sparkling in the sun,
The linen's snowy white.

And from the kitchen comes the smell
Of what her hands prepare . . .
A turkey browning to a turn,
Pies baked with loving care.

The house is spotless as can be;
The panes of windows glow,
And Grandpa's sweeping from the steps
A trace of feather snow.

This is their day when once again
The children will be here,
Gathered around the table's rim
From places far and near.

And when the quiet moment comes,
When heads are bowed to pray,
They'll thank the Lord for family ties
And for Thanksgiving Day.

AUTUMN LEAVES AND LAUGHTER *by Randy Van Beek.*
Image from Applejack Art Partners

THE PRAYER WHEEL

by Lad Moore

It was Stell on the phone again," my wife explained. "She says she's counting the days until we get there."

Every Thanksgiving was the same. The extended families awaited the call from Granny Stell that told of special plans for the year's most celebratory meal. The conversation always ended the same reassuring way. "No," she would say, "you dare not bring a thing."

It was like a migration of wayward birds returning to their famed Capistrano. From all across the country, family members descended on Hardesty Farm in rural Altus, Arkansas. Early arrivers got the choice bedrooms—the foot-draggers having to settle for cots and pallets. . . .

Grandpa Hardesty always said grace. It was as if he spent the preceding twelve months keeping notes for just this occasion. He made sure each family member was represented in what we called his prayer wheel—citing an event in our lives during the year. Maybe it was nothing more than little Archie's "C" in arithmetic, or Aunt Flossie's recovery from a bout with the croup. Perhaps it was just thanks for Jim's new job, or—ahem—acknowledgment of "Old Maid" Ruth's surprise honeymoon.

We all felt special when Grandpa got to our name in the wheel. Not so much for what he said, but because we knew he had cared enough to keep track of us all for another year. Eventually, Grandpa worked through the entire list—despite the occasional impatient eye that would peek at the waiting vittles and stir a resurgence of salivary juices.

"Amen, great God and Jehovah. Amen."

The blessing was over. Like spontaneous combustion, clangs from the arming of utensils engulfed the room. Grandpa carved the turkey as dervish-like hands passed the platters in both directions. Erupting conversations ran left, right, and sideways. Words and sentences, pent-up from the long prayer, gushed out in unison.

And so we carried on, year after year. One particular Thanksgiving sticks out in my mind, though. After the long prayer wheel concluded, the table erupted into serving and eating. Someone's voice carried loud and clear. "Would you look at these lovely peas!"

Another gave stern directions. "Jaime, take some of this corn. It's Grandpa Hardesty's own."

Aunt Flossie, a proud cook in her own right, offered a veiled challenge. "Stell," she asked, "did you change something in this giblet gravy? Do I taste oregano?"

Occupying a third of my plate were Stell's prize-winning purple-hull peas, slow simmered with bacon, peppers, and a hint of sugar. Stell's rules forbade the buying of shelled peas. Family members earned the right to eat peas by shelling them first. As a child in my summers at Hardesty Farm, we shelled peas together in family ritual.

I remember how Stell formed a bowl in her lap with her apron to cradle the peas. The hulls were tossed onto a newspaper spread on the floor. Guy Lombardo's music paced the activity, his sounds wandering our way from a giant Philco radio that was the nesting place for Grandpa's aromatic pipe tobaccos.

To sop up the pot liquor, there was scalded cornbread emblazoned with shards of cayenne peppers. To help tame it, it received a cardio-risky triple patty of butter.

We heaped our plates with turkey and sage dressing, along with mayonnaise-drenched salad. The delicate flowers on Stell's best china were completely obscured by the overhang of double helpings.

For dessert, there were the Thanksgiving Trinity pies—pecan, pumpkin, and lemon icebox. As a special temptation, Stell had also prepared the same coconut cake that once earned her a blue ribbon at the Ozark Fair. It was special because she grated a fresh coconut herself—

Photograph by Luca Trovato/Botanica/Jupiter Images

merging it into a secret-ingredient icing. It was also her custom—I never knew its origin—to hide a dime somewhere in the cake. Whoever found it presumably would have good luck.

Everyone took a piece, but with the first bite, we all stopped chewing. Large chunks fell from wide-open mouths. The cake held the unmistakable taste of soap! All conversation stopped, the soft radio music coming from the living room heard for the first time that day.

Stell first objected, then denied. She got up quickly and went over to the sink, where the coconut still lay. Missing was the big bar of Ivory soap from its place on the dish above the faucet. Her face was ablaze with embarrassment.

"Oh my stars . . ." she said under her breath.

Each of us in turn used humor to lighten our reaction.

"That doesn't compare with the time Grandpa forgot to remove the pellets from those pheasants," I said. "Near 'bout broke my only gold tooth!"

"Remember when Aunt Flossie made that upside-down cake that Jaime said he couldn't tell up from down?" asked Jim.

Eventually, we pried a smile from Stell's embarrassed lips. Even Flossie showed restraint over the champion cook's error, but I noticed a hint of satisfaction in her partial smile. The rest of us just smiled, already looking forward to next Thanksgiving. Grandpa had been seen making a note of the event. It would undoubtedly reappear somewhere in next year's wheel.

Oh—and in all the fuss, nobody found the dime.

TRADITIONS
Carol Hammond

Our lives are punctuated by celebrations. Traditions that live from year to year—family to family—secure our place in family history. Thanksgiving is the granddaddy of these occasions. I love the knowledge that my grandmother stuffed her turkey with the same dressing recipe that I am using today. That my great-grandparents used some of the same dishes that my grandchildren will eat off of today. That my sisters—scattered across the country—will be making the same frozen fruit salad and cranberry nut bread that my mother always made.

As I stand in my Florida kitchen, I imagine them in their kitchens preparing their feasts and I feel close to them. Thankful for them and the rest of our family and all they mean to me. As we share our customs, traditions, and stories with our children and grandchildren, these things will live on in their hearts also, strengthening all our family ties.

Thanksgiving lives in our hearts and can be celebrated anywhere. "It's in our hearts and in our souls." Whether we are at the beach, in the desert, on the Kansas plains, or in a busy city, we are all united at Thanksgiving.

What began many years ago with handmade pinecone turkeys and frozen fruit salad really does last a lifetime . . . and beyond.

The Ardsley House, Catskill Mountains Park and Preserve, New York. Photograph by Carr Clifton

Family Recipes

BUTTERNUT SQUASH AND PARSNIP BAKED PASTA

1   tablespoon olive oil
1   cup finely chopped onion
¼   teaspoon crushed red pepper
2   garlic cloves, minced
2   cups (½-inch) cubed peeled,
        seeded butternut squash
1   cup chopped parsnip
1   tablespoon chopped fresh or
        1 teaspoon dried rubbed sage
1   tablespoon chopped fresh or
        1 teaspoon dried parsley
¼   teaspoon ground nutmeg
¼   teaspoon ground allspice
½   teaspoon salt, divided
½   teaspoon black pepper, divided
2   cups uncooked penne pasta
½   cup (2 ounces) grated fresh
        Parmesan cheese, divided
    Cooking spray
1½ tablespoons butter
2   tablespoons all-purpose flour
1   cup heavy cream

Preheat oven to 375°F. Heat oil in a large non-stick skillet over medium-high heat. Add onion, red pepper, and garlic; sauté 3 minutes. Add squash and parsnip; sauté 10 minutes. Stir in sage, parsley, nutmeg, allspice, ¼ teaspoon salt, and ¼ teaspoon black pepper; remove from heat.

Cook pasta according to package directions. Drain in a colander over a bowl, reserving 1 cup cooking liquid. Combine squash mixture, pasta, and ¼ cup cheese in an 11 x 7-inch baking dish coated with cooking spray, tossing gently to combine.

In a medium saucepan over medium heat, melt the butter. Add flour; cook 3 minutes, stirring constantly with a whisk. Add cream; cook 5 minutes, stirring constantly with a whisk. Gradually add reserved cooking liquid; cook 2 minutes or until thick, stirring constantly with a whisk. Add ¼ teaspoon salt and ¼ teaspoon pepper.

Pour cream mixture over pasta mixture; sprinkle with ¼ cup cheese. Bake for 30 minutes or until lightly browned. Makes 4 servings.

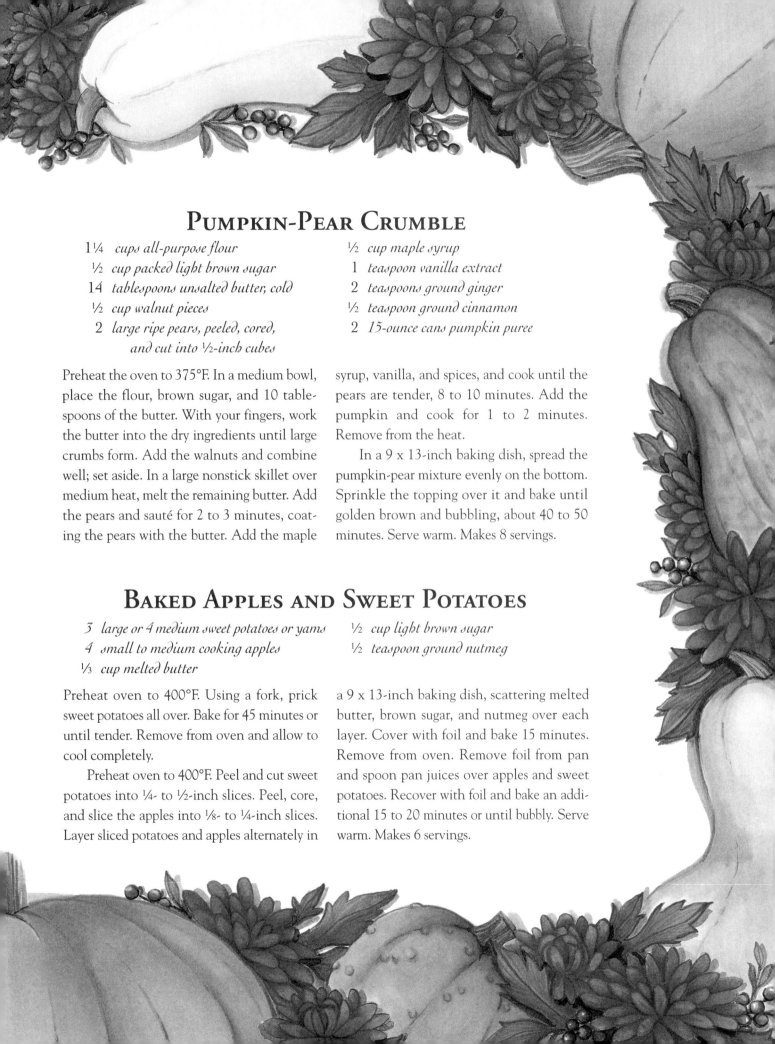

PUMPKIN-PEAR CRUMBLE

1¼   cups all-purpose flour
½   cup packed light brown sugar
14   tablespoons unsalted butter, cold
½   cup walnut pieces
2   large ripe pears, peeled, cored,
        and cut into ½-inch cubes

½   cup maple syrup
1   teaspoon vanilla extract
2   teaspoons ground ginger
½   teaspoon ground cinnamon
2   15-ounce cans pumpkin puree

Preheat the oven to 375°F. In a medium bowl, place the flour, brown sugar, and 10 tablespoons of the butter. With your fingers, work the butter into the dry ingredients until large crumbs form. Add the walnuts and combine well; set aside. In a large nonstick skillet over medium heat, melt the remaining butter. Add the pears and sauté for 2 to 3 minutes, coating the pears with the butter. Add the maple syrup, vanilla, and spices, and cook until the pears are tender, 8 to 10 minutes. Add the pumpkin and cook for 1 to 2 minutes. Remove from the heat.

In a 9 x 13-inch baking dish, spread the pumpkin-pear mixture evenly on the bottom. Sprinkle the topping over it and bake until golden brown and bubbling, about 40 to 50 minutes. Serve warm. Makes 8 servings.

BAKED APPLES AND SWEET POTATOES

3   large or 4 medium sweet potatoes or yams
4   small to medium cooking apples
⅓   cup melted butter

½   cup light brown sugar
½   teaspoon ground nutmeg

Preheat oven to 400°F. Using a fork, prick sweet potatoes all over. Bake for 45 minutes or until tender. Remove from oven and allow to cool completely.

Preheat oven to 400°F. Peel and cut sweet potatoes into ¼- to ½-inch slices. Peel, core, and slice the apples into ⅛- to ¼-inch slices. Layer sliced potatoes and apples alternately in a 9 x 13-inch baking dish, scattering melted butter, brown sugar, and nutmeg over each layer. Cover with foil and bake 15 minutes. Remove from oven. Remove foil from pan and spoon pan juices over apples and sweet potatoes. Recover with foil and bake an additional 15 to 20 minutes or until bubbly. Serve warm. Makes 6 servings.

Save Room

Joanna Fuchs

As meals go, Thanksgiving dinner
Is always a feast—a five star winner.
Here comes the salad, dressed just right,
The golden brown turkey—a savory delight;

The stuffing now, and then the gravy,
The jello mold, all wiggly and wavy.
Take some cranberry sauce and candied yams.
Is there room for fresh made rolls and jams?

More dishes tempt me; ah, but I
Must save some room for pumpkin pie!

Pumpkin bars and
pumpkin bread
And spicy pumpkin pies
And pumpkin puddings,
pumpkin cakes
Oh, how they appetize!
—CRAIG E. SATHOFF

Photograph by Jessie Walker

WISHBONE SCIENCE

N. V. Bennett

It was a cold and windy fall day as we stepped onto the frozen road in our itchy Sunday best. Most Sundays we would have whined, but on certain occasions, when that special aroma wafted from the stovepipes straight to our noses, we were too excited to protest. Instead, we raced across the winding roads to our grandparents' house for dinner, autumn leaves swirling around our feet as we ran. With the onset of darkness, cornstalks left standing in the fields swayed ominously, crackling in the gusty breezes and sounding like the rustle of wild animals. Undeterred, we hurried on, for the wind also carried the smell of Grandmother's turkey.

The meal itself was always a grand affair: roasted corn, oozing with butter; mashed potatoes—skins off for special occasions; dill and sweet pickles of all sorts and sizes; white rolls and tons of gravy; and, of course, mushed-up turnips for my mother and grandmother.

The turkey made a resounding thump as it was hoisted from the stove to the table. And when Grandfather began to carve, the juices flowed down and across the blue serving plate. We salivated in anticipation.

Because I was his favorite, Grandfather always saved the wishbone for me.

The science of wishbone preparation was no simple matter. You couldn't take a fresh one and make your wish right then and there. You had to age it first. That meant drying it carefully, turning it daily, and not forgetting it on the pantry shelf or fridge top. Timing was everything. Too long and it would shard off—you would have trouble making a clear break. Too soft and it would be rubbery and twisty, and no matter how hard you tried, you could not bend it to break properly.

There was also the important choice of the right partner to break it with. My parents rarely participated. Mom thought the idea was paramount to germ spreading, a regular Typhoid Mary in the making. If she found my wishbone, it would end up in the garbage can, and I would have to wait till the next turkey dinner and then hide it better.

Grandfather was a sport, but he had tough, gnarled sailor fingers, which sometimes didn't fit; and Grandmother's blue-veined knitting hands were too busy for games. This left me with my siblings to choose from.

Diplomacy dictated that I ask Cathy, the

eldest sister, first. I was glad when she said no, for she did not present much of a partner. She neither believed nor disbelieved in such things as luck and wishbones. Who would want to

share a wishbone and possibly a wish with a disbeliever?

My second eldest sister was Pat. I often didn't bother to ask her either. Pat simply couldn't be bothered—too busy with boys or dreaming of rock stars—and she hated turkey.

Brother Ken was to be avoided at all costs. I hid my precious wishbone if I saw him coming. He would twist my arm in half as well as the wishbone, and if I refused to hand it over or say "Uncle," he might give me a snake bite.

That left the next in line: Jeanette. She was still of an age where she believed in wishbones, good-luck charms, and giving a smaller, younger sister a fair chance by using her weaker hand.

Now, with a family of my own, I have become the cooker of the turkey. My husband does the oven calculations and carves the sacred bird.

Perhaps I have grown too old for childish wishes; perhaps by now I might have other bones to pick. But I still remember Grandpa, who was never too old for magic; and so each time I cook a turkey, I secret away the wishbone and wrap it in a clean paper towel. After it dries, I summon my daughters to join fingers, close their eyes, and pull in hopes of a clean break and the chance to wish.

Costume Designer
Betty Isler

Again we face Thanksgiving Day
With offspring in the fourth grade play,
And I could shake each Pilgrim father
For all the worry and the bother
He has bequeathed this addled parent,
Who wilts before this task inherent
In fashioning this permanent press
Into Pricilla's homespun dress,
Or shaping good John Alden's hat
From bits of space age this and that.
As muttering I fuss and toil
With buckles made of kitchen foil,
Or starching squares of dacron sheet
Into quaint kerchiefs, white and neat,
I wonder if those women found
Such problems being cloaked and gowned.
Methinks it harder now to fake them
Than starting out from scratch to make them.

Captured Spirit
Alice Leedy Mason

The children speak. They play a part
And history takes the form of art.
Caught in the spell of "play-pretend,"
The audience sees what may have been.

They live again with men of old . . .
Indian brave, Pilgrim bold,
Sharing gifts for the common good,
Knowing the strength of brotherhood.

In simple words, spoken well,
The past rings out like a golden bell.
Seedtime, harvest, friendship, prayer,
Familiar scenes are captured there.

The play is done . . . the curtain falls.
Performance merits curtain calls.
A backward glance has come and gone
But the Pilgrim spirit lingers on.

Finally on Thanksgiving

Patricia Penton Leimbach

"First there was the ship, and then there was the storm. And the first baby was born, and they got off on the rock. And then they met the Indians and got the corn, and then they had the first Thanksgiving," wrote Teddy when he was six. Thanksgiving at six is pictures of people strangely dressed in black and gray with buckles on their shoes.

It is the day the relatives come with their damp, unwelcome kisses, the table is stretched to fill the dining room, and dinner is forever getting served. I remember it all, and the changing impressions . . . wishing I were old enough to sit at the big table instead of the smaller one at the side, wishing that my pinecone turkeys would stand more firmly in their pipe-cleaner legs.

Setting the table carefully with the heirloom linens and the stemmed goblets was a joy of growing older. . . . It mattered little that the china didn't all match, or that the goblets were chipped. In some odd way, it assured me that our "peasant" existence was only a façade, that behind it all we were gentry born to the silver spoon.

When the food finally came and we assembled about our round table, there was a smug sense of unity and well-being. The plates were never big enough, and the gravy ran over the corn while the pickled peach rolled into the mashed potatoes. Everyone exclaimed about so much food, and where would they put it all, and why couldn't their stomachs hold more.

Thanksgiving in the teen years was washing dishes for hours, then trudging through wet pastures with a swain who thought Thanksgiving was a hunter's holiday. Eventually, Thanksgiving was homecoming and bringing your roommate. It was looking for the action in the hometown and working on term papers and going back to college disappointed but never admitting it.

Having a fiancé at Thanksgiving was finding that suddenly the house was too small and the family too big and too noisy, and there was no place to be alone. Then Thanksgiving was "over the river and . . ." down the freeway to Grandmother's house and taking your place at the stove and understanding at last what took so long.

And all through those years, giving thanks was something superimposed on the holiday at the last minute when the turkey steamed on the platter, like a salt shaker you've forgotten and jump up to bring to the table.

If, however, you are among the blessed who cling to the land, there comes finally a year when the full realization of Thanksgiving is upon you, when you see back through the harvest of autumn to the cultivation of summer, to the tilling of spring. You hold the fruit, sense the plant, and bless the seed.

You kneel before the altar of weather—rain and sun and wind and frost. You rejoice in technology; you sing hymns to good health; you praise God for a husband, children, workmen who are skilled and faithful in their labor. You thank the Lord for food and the privilege of producing it. Now, at last, you understand about the ship and the corn and the people with buckles on their shoes. Finally you have a thanks-giving—and on it you superimpose a holiday.

Photograph by Jessie Walker

The Landing

Felicia D. Hemans

The breaking waves dashed high
    On a stern and rock-bound coast,
And the woods against a stormy sky
    Their giant branches tossed;

And the heavy night hung dark
    The hills and waters o'er,
When a band of exiles moored their bark
    On the wild New England shore.

Not as the conqueror comes,
    They, the true-hearted came;
Not with the roll of the stirring drums,
    And the trumpet that sings of fame;

Not as the flying come,
    In silence and in fear;—
They shook the depths of the desert gloom
    With their hymns of lofty cheer.

Amidst the storm they sang,
    And the stars heard, and the sea;
And the sounding aisles of the dim woods rang
    To the anthem of the free.

The ocean eagle soared
    From his nest by the white wave's foam,
And the rocking pines of the forest roared—
    This was their welcome home.

There were men with hoary hair
    Amidst that Pilgrim band:
Why had they come to wither there,
    Away from their childhood's land?

There was woman's fearless eye,
    Lit by her deep love's truth;
There was manhood's brow serenely high,
    And the fiery heart of youth.

What sought they thus afar?
    Bright jewels of the mine?
The wealth of seas, the spoils of war?—
    They sought a faith's pure shrine!

Ay, call it holy ground,
    The soil where first they trod.
They have left unstained what there they found—
    Freedom to worship God.

The First Thanksgiving

Reid Crowell

The Indian summer haze was gone, and frost
Had come to paint the hills with scarlet brush;
The barking of a fox came from the wood,
And cornstalks rattled in November's hush.
The gates of the stockade were safely shut
Against the yet untraversed wilderness;
The Pilgrims bowed in prayer around the board . . .
They broke their bread and asked for God to bless

The plates of corn, browned turkeys from the wild,
The blue-sheened grapes, and slabs of venison . . .
These proofs that He had blessed their hopeful toil,
And given them His fruitful benison.
The twilight came to end their day of prayer . . .
Beyond the virgin clearing they had hewn,
New England skies, above the darkened ridge,
Grew warm with light where sailed the harvest moon.

Upon Landing

William Bradford

Being thus arrived and brought safe to land, they fell upon their knees and blessed the God of heaven Who had brought them over the vast and furious ocean and delivered them from all the perils and miseries thereof, again to set their feet on the firm and stable earth . . . Being thus past the vast ocean, and a sea of troubles before in their preparation, they had now no friends to welcome them, no inns to entertain or refresh their weather-beaten bodies, no houses or much less towns to repair to, to seek for succor. It is recorded in Scripture as a mercy to the apostle and his ship-wrecked company that the barbarians showed them no small kindness in refreshing them; but these savage barbarians, when they met them, were readier to fill their sides full of arrows . . . And for the season, it was winter, and they that know the winters of that country know them to be sharp and violent and subject to cruel and fierce storms, dangerous to travel to known places, much more to search an unknown coast.

Besides, what could they see but a hideous and desolate wilderness, full of wild beasts and wild men? And what multitudes of them there might be they knew not . . . Which way so ever they turned their eyes (save upwards to the heavens) they could have little solace or content in respect of any outward objects. For summer being done, all things stand upon them with a weather-beaten face; and the whole country, full of woods and thickets, represented a savage and wild hue. If they looked behind them, there was the mighty ocean they had passed and was now as a main bar and gulf to separate them from all the civil parts of the world. . . .

What could sustain them but the spirit of God and His grace? May not and ought not the children of these fathers rightly say: "Our fathers were Englishmen which came over this great ocean and were ready to perish in the wilderness; but they cried unto the Lord, and He heard their voices and looked on their adversity. Let them therefore praise the Lord because He is good and His mercies endure forever. . . ."

Plymouth, Massachusetts. Photograph by Pixtal/SuperStock

Thankful, No Matter What

Pamela Kennedy

How easy it is to give thanks when life is going smoothly, when we see answers to our prayers, and when our days are filled with sunshine. The more difficult task is to express gratitude when we're facing opposition, God appears to be silent, or storm clouds darken our skies. This beautiful hymn of thanksgiving, written almost four hundred years ago, is a perfect reminder that real gratitude is all about recognizing our blessings especially when they seem obscured by our circumstances.

Early in the seventeenth century, Martin Rinkart, a newly ordained Lutheran minister, was assigned to serve the congregation in his hometown of Eilenberg, Germany. A haven for refugees fleeing the violence of the Thirty Years' War, Eilenberg quickly became overcrowded and undersupplied with food, sanitary facilities, and medical care. Before long, the walled city became a city of death. Plagues and pestilence raced through the streets. Other ministers and priests died or fled, leaving Rinkart to tend to his ever-dwindling and increasingly needy parishioners. Faced with staggering losses, including members of his own family, there were months when the weary pastor conducted up to forty-five funerals a day.

Threats from within the city were not his only concern. Warring armies periodically stormed into Eilenberg demanding tribute and further depleting the city's meager resources. At one point, faced with almost certain death because they could not meet the demands of an angry general, the desperate citizens gathered in the city square. Under Rinkart's direction, they knelt on the paving stones as he prayed before their enemy, "Come, my children, we can find no mercy with man; let us take refuge with God." Following this brief prayer, he led his little flock in the singing of a familiar hymn. Stunned by such courage and faith, the general withdrew, sparing the city.

But their respite was brief. Shortages of food and water constantly challenged Eilenberg's citizens. Still, Rinkart would not surrender to despair. Bereft of almost every earthly resource, the faithful pastor called upon his wealth of creativity and hope to compose over sixty hymns, intending to turn the eyes of his people from their own poverty to the power and love of God. He encouraged them to see that their circumstances were temporary, while God's blessings were eternal, transcending earth's difficulties.

Martin Rinkart discovered the secret that true thankfulness requires a "no matter what" mindset. His famous hymn, "Now Thank We All Our God," declares across the centuries that our Heavenly Father has accomplished wondrous things, blessing each of us with countless gifts of love. This Thanksgiving, may your heart be filled with gratitude in the midst of whatever circumstances you face. And may you also discover the grace to give thanks . . . no matter what.

Now Thank We All Our God

by Martin Rinkart, melody by Johann Cruger

1. Now thank we all our God With heart and hands and voic - es,
2. O may this boun- teous God Thro' all our life be near us,
3. All praise and thanks to God The Fa - ther now be giv - en,

Who won-drous things hath done, In Whom His world re - joic - es;
With ev - er joy - ful hearts And bless - ed peace to cheer us;
The Son, and Him Who reigns With Them in high - est heav - en,

Who, from our moth - er's arms, Hath blest us on our way
And keep us in His grace, And guide us when per - plexed,
The one e - ter - nal God, Whom earth and heav'n a - dore;

With count - less gifts of love, And still is ours to - day.
And free us from all ills now, In this world and the next.
For thus it was, is now, And shall be ev - er - more.

THANKFUL
Patience Strong

Thankful may I ever be for everything that God bestows. Thankful for the joys and sorrows, for the blessings and the blows. Thankful for the wisdom gained through hardship and adversity. Thankful for the undertones as well as for the melody.

Thankful may I ever be for benefits both great and small—and never fail in gratitude for that divinest gift of all: the love of friends that I have known in times of failures and success. O may the first prayer of the day be always one of thankfulness.

Thanksgiving for No
Carol Bessent Hayman

This year I thank You, Lord, for things
    that seemed not given.
It is so easy to give thanks for food,
For shelter, for loved ones near:
These I can touch and see.
I give You thanks instead for all the no's You have said.
I am a wilful one, inclined to feel I know the way ahead.
Thank You for keeping these poor stumbling feet
From all the worldly pleasures they could find.
Thank You for guiding me along a path,
Much harder, Lord, than I thought I could climb,
And thank You most of all for saying no! when
    I would faint and fall,
To let another shoulder my heart's load.
You gave me strength, You taught me patience, love;
And so, on this Thanksgiving Day,
Thank You, Lord, for every time
    this wonderful, learning year
When You said no.

Photograph by William H. Johnson

THROUGH MY WINDOW

POTLUCK PERILS
Pamela Kennedy

On a balmy early November day we mingled with friends and newcomers after Sunday morning services. Although our Hawaiian weather belied the season, it was just a few weeks until Thanksgiving and plans were underway for the traditional all-church holiday potluck dinner. As my husband and I started for our car, a young couple passed us, deep in earnest conversation. I couldn't help but notice the concern in the woman's voice.

"Sure I'd love to go, but I don't have a clue what you make for a potluck dinner around here. Besides, the only thing I'm really good at cooking is frozen pizza!" I smiled remembering just such a conversation my husband and I had several decades earlier.

The first time we were invited to a Thanksgiving potluck dinner I was a new bride with one cookbook, a wedding gift from my favorite aunt. It looked great on the bookshelf in our apartment, but I had never actually opened its pristine red and white plaid cover prior to the potluck invitation. My culinary creations to that point centered on ground beef variations I remembered from my mother's repertoire and salads created from whatever produce happened to be on sale at the local market. But our church was planning a big holiday potluck, and I couldn't

wait to delve into the mysteries of my new cookbook. Just leafing through its pages made my mouth water. The only problem was that there were so many recipes that involved mysterious procedures. What, for instance, was the difference between mincing and dicing? I knew how to fold laundry, but how was I supposed to fold beaten egg whites? And if I reduced something to thicken it, could I expand it by reversing the process?

The Ladies' Guild, sponsors of the potluck, had supposedly lessened the stress of the cooks by assigning categories according to one's last name. H-M brought vegetable dishes, so there I was, a K, madly poring through everything from artichokes to zucchini. My husband, vegephobic in his early years, vetoed most of my choices. He turned down all manner of beans, cabbages, most root vegetables, eggplants, squashes of every hue, onions, green peppers, and peas. Finally, after much debate, we decided upon "Dixie Bake"—a concoction of mashed sweet potatoes, eggs, honey, and pecans. It really resembled a dessert more than a side dish, but it met my requirement of easy preparation and my husband's of tasting nothing at all like a vegetable.

Thanksgiving afternoon we showed up bearing our offering for the buffet table. We tenderly set it down amidst the dozens of other dishes, not unlike parents leaving their firstborn at kindergarten. How would our little "Dixie Bake" fare next to the creations prepared by far more experienced cooks? When long lines of diners came to fill their plates, would our sweet potatoes be chosen? Or would they languish in their casserole dish, passed over for more exotic fare like Zucchini Parmesan or Green Beans Almondine? We feared hearing that dreaded culinary critique:

"EEEWWWW! I'm not touching that with a ten foot pole!" Or being subjected to that worst of all potluck perils—retrieving from the buffet table a dish nearly as full as when we brought it! Happily, none of these occurred. In fact, I almost blushed when the gentleman ahead of me scooped up a huge spoonful of my "Dixie Bake," plopped it on his plate, and announced, "Look here, Pearl, I haven't had this since my mamma made it for me years ago!" Prompted by this expression of enthusiasm, my husband even took a small helping. I smiled and opted for the Zucchini, something I was sure I'd never see at our house. The only perils we really suffered that Thanksgiving were the pains and discomfort caused by overeating. That's the other thing about potlucks. No matter your good intentions, you can't just take a small plate of food when faced with such a plethora of delicious choices.

And don't even think about not going back for seconds! We waddled out to our car, carrying our empty casserole dish and about five extra pounds apiece!

I can't count the number of potlucks we've attended in the almost forty years since that first one. These days my red and white plaid cookbook is held together with duct tape and many of the pages are smudged and spattered. I can mince, dice, reduce, and fold with ease, and my husband has even learned to enjoy quite a few vegetables. But when Thanksgiving comes around and we're invited to a potluck I still make at least one small batch of "Dixie Bake," just for old times. Those early potluck perils seem far behind me now . . . all except one. Despite my best efforts and ongoing resolution, at the end of the annual potluck I still inevitably suffer from the distress of overeating!

Thanksgiving Service

Harriet Whipple

In the quiet church we gather
On a cold November day;
We listen to the organ
And bow our heads to pray.
A special warmth within us
Is the gratitude we feel
And thanksgiving for the blessings
The heart and mind reveal.

We think about the wonders
That every season brings,
And we are very thankful
For so many precious things.
For freedom in our country
And its beauty all around;
For the right to meet together
And the solace we have found.

For all our friends and dear ones
And the love in which we share;
For the bounty of the harvest
And to nature everywhere.
For the gift of life so precious
And our valued senses too;
For rest and food and talents
And work that we may do.

For music, art, and poetry
And books that we may read;
For inventions that are useful
And the many things we need.
For those men of dedication
Who help us all so much
And those with special insight
Who add a loving touch.

For faith and inspiration;
For hope and courage too;
For the Bible that will guide us
in whatever we may do.
For all this we are grateful . . .
In prayer and song this way
We offer thanks together
In the house of God today.

All Praise to God
John Milton

Let us, with a gladsome mind,
Praise the Lord, for He is kind:

For His mercies aye endure,
Ever faithful, ever sure.

Let us blaze His name abroad,
For of gods He is the God:

He, with all-commanding might,
Filled the new-made world with light:

All things living He doth feed,
His full hand supplies their need:

He His chosen race did bless
In the wasteful wilderness:

Let us then with gladsome mind
Praise the Lord, for He is kind.

Selection
John Greenleaf Whittier

Heap high the farmer's wintry hoard!
Heap high the golden corn!
No richer gift has autumn poured
From out her lavish horn.

Let other lands exulting glean
The apple from the pine,
The orange from its glossy green,
The cluster from the vine.

But let the good old corn adorn
The hills our fathers trod;
Still let us, for His golden corn,
Send up our thanks to God.

Photograph by Dennis Frates

Giving Thanks
Anonymous

For the hay and the corn and wheat that is reaped,
For the labor well done and the barns that are heaped,
For the sun and the dew and the sweet honeycomb,
For the rose and the song and the harvest brought home—

Thanksgiving! Thanksgiving!

For the trade and the skill and the wealth in our land,
For the cunning and strength of the workingman's hand,
For the good that our artists and poets have taught,
For the friendship that hope and affection have brought—

Thanksgiving! Thanksgiving!

For the homes that with purest affection are blest,
For the season of plenty and well deserved rest,
For our country extending from sea to sea,
The land that is known as the "Land of the Free"—

Thanksgiving! Thanksgiving!

Come, ye thankful people, come,
Raise the song of harvest home.
All is safely gathered in,
Ere the winter storms begin.
God, our Maker, doth provide
For our wants to be supplied;
Come to God's own temple, come;
Raise the song of harvest home.
—HENRY ALFORD

AUTUMN SOLITUDE *by Randy Van Beek. Image from*
Applejack Art Partners

Thanksgiving

F. R. Havergal

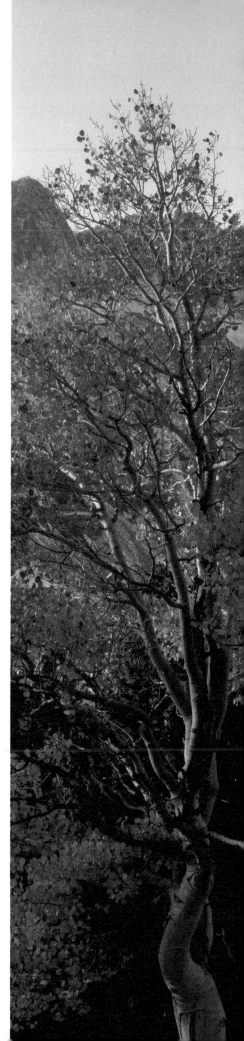

Thanks be to God!
    to whom Earth owes
Sunshine and breeze,
The heath-clad hill,
    the vale's repose,
Streamlet and seas,
The snowdrop and
    the summer rose,
The many-voiced trees.

Thanks for the darkness
    that reveals
Night's starry dower;
And for the sable
    cloud that heals
Each fevered flower;
And for the rushing
    storm that peals
Our weakness and Thy power.

Thanks for the
    sweetly-lingering might
In music's tone;
For paths of knowledge,
    whose calm light
Is all Thine own;
For thoughts that at the Infinite
Fold their bright wings alone.

Yet thanks that silence
    oft may flow
In dewlike store;
Thanks for the
    mysteries that show

How small our lore;
Thanks that we here
    so little know
And trust Thee all the more!

Thanks for the
    gladness that entwines
Our path below;
Each sunrise that incarnadines
The cold, still snow;
Thanks for the light
    of love which shines
With brightest earthly glow.

Thanks for Thine own
    thrice-blessed Word,
And Sabbath rest;
Thanks for the hope
    of glory stored
In mansions blest;
Thanks for the Spirit's
    comfort poured
Into the trembling breast.

Thanks, more thanks,
    to Him ascend,
Who died to win
Our life, and every trophy rend
From Death and Sin;
Till, when the thanks
    of earth shall end,
The thanks of Heaven begin.

Wheeler Peak, Great Basin National Park, Nevada.
Photograph © George Ward/drr.net